garden
mosaics

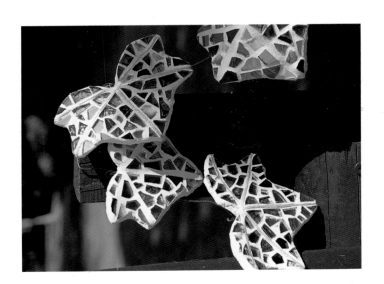

garden
mosaics

25 step-by-step projects
for your outdoor room

Becky Paton

CICO BOOKS
LONDON NEW YORK

The Author

Becky Paton studied Art and Design at Chelsea School of Art in London, where she specialized in mosaic-making. She now works as a mosaic artist in the UK and Norway undertaking public, community, and private art commissions, and her most recent public art commission was the mosaic name plate for the V&A Museum of Childhood in London. Becky also teaches and exhibits both in her hometown of Oxford and overseas.

First published in 2004 by CICO Books
This edition published in 2010 by CICO Books
an imprint of Ryland Peters & Small
519 Broadway, 5th Floor, New York, NY 10012
20–21 Jockey's Fields, London, WC1R 4BW

www.cicobooks.com

10 9 8 7 6 5 4 3

A CIP catalog record for this book is available from the Library of Congress and the British Library.

ISBN: 978 1 907030 32 1
(Previous ISBN: 978 1 903116 92 0)

Printed in China

Editor: Robin Gurdon
Photography: Tino Tedaldi
Styling: Julie Hailey
Design: Christine Wood

Acknowledgments

My love and thanks goes firstly to my family for their constant support and encouragement. Special thanks to Oliver and Isabel for giving up so much of their summer holiday so Mummy could work, and to Chris for holding the fort. A huge thank you to Cindy, Tino, Georgina, Julie, Robin, and everybody else at CICO Books—working with you has been an absolute pleasure.

Many thanks to Sarah and Nigel, Karen and Alex, Oliver and Virginie, Tom, Sue, and Jessica for allowing us to use their beautiful gardens and being so hospitable, we really appreciated it. Thank you, Nina, for letting me rummage in your new house and take away the former owner's rubbish, it was gold dust to me!

A very special thank you to Ken at Reed Harris, Mike at The Mosaic Shop, and Patti at Happycraft for being so generous and supportive, I hope you like the results. Big thanks to Ingrid Gaitet for allowing us to photograph her beautiful spheres in the birdbath and garden bowl and also to Julie Walters for her intricate "Number 74."

Last, but certainly not least, many, many thanks to East Oxford Mosaic Workshop for being a constant source of inspiration and a joy to be part of these last few years.

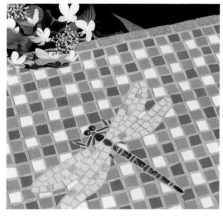

contents

Introduction 6

MATERIALS AND TECHNIQUES 8
Tesserae 8
Cutting Tiles 10
Mixing Sand and Cement 12
Direct Method 13
Mixing Grout 14
Using Grout 15
Tools 16
Other Techniques 18
Indirect or Reverse Method 19

POTS AND PLANTERS 20
Ivy-leaf Hanging Pot 22
Recycled Concrete Planter 26
Two-handled Urn 28
Cone Planter 32

GARDEN ADDITIONS 36
Fountain 38
Children's Footprints 42
House Number 48
Birdbath 52
Summertime Sphere 54
Suncatcher 58
Ammonite Stepping Stone 62
Shoal of Fish 66
Sparkling Fish 72
Ivy Vine 76
Butterfly on a Stone 80
Ladybug Stone 84
Bird Feeder 86
Dragonfly 88

MOSAIC LIVING 92
Gingham Table Top 94
Honeycomb Tray 98
Place Mats 102
Coasters 106
Fern Plate 108
Plant Shelf 110
Candle Holder 112

Templates 116
Index 128

introduction

The art of mosaic is one of the most durable art forms known to man and certainly one of the most diverse—how many other mediums can be used as functional paving, or placed in a frame to be hung on the wall?

The first known mosaics, found in the Middle East, were clay cones stuck into wet mud. The Greeks developed the technique with pebbles, the Romans refined the art further using cubes cut from stone, and the Byzantines introduced glass. Now, almost any material, from sea shells to old coins, is used in an art form whose boundaries continue to be pushed.

Mosaics work well in all exterior settings, from the country garden to the courtyard, or the sleek urban landscape. They add color, vibrancy, and individuality. The permanence of a mosaic complements the changing seasons and adds an alternative focal point that will be appreciated all year long.

This book concentrates on 25 mosaics for the garden using many different techniques, and a diverse range of materials. With projects for all abilities ranging from drinks coasters, which would be perfect for a beginner, to a sculptural fish, which will appeal to the more advanced, my aim is to encourage experimentation that results in stunning works of art.

I hope you will enjoy making the projects in this book as much as I have enjoyed creating them for you. Feel free to change the materials or colors I have used—remember: play around, and continue to push those boundaries!

WORKING SPACE

Before undertaking a mosaic, it is important to give some thought to your working environment. First, find a good, stable work surface that will be large enough for the mosaic, all the tiles you are using, the required tools and adhesives, as well as this book if you are following one of the projects.

Because chippings from both the glass and ceramic tiles can be very sharp, choose an area in which you can contain them, and sweep or vacuum when you are finished. If space is limited, or you are concerned about your children's or pets' feet, then a good solution is to cut tiles inside a large cardboard box—most of the chips will fall into the bottom, containing the mess. Make sure your working space is well ventilated, as grouts and cements can be very dusty in their dry form; it can sometimes be sensible to wear a mask.

When working in the garden, as I have done for these projects, keep a keen eye on the weather! Rain on a half-completed mosaic could ruin it. Strong direct sunlight can also cause problems: if grouting, the drying time will be dramatically reduced, so keep a keen eye; also avoid putting sand and cement out to dry in this weather as it will almost certainly crack it.

To complete a mosaic can take from as little as a few hours (very rare!) up to some days. Don't be put off by the timing, just ensure that your working space can be either left intact or easily tidied up and reassembled when needed. Organization is the key, both to making a mosaic, and the space in which you work.

materials and techniques

TESSERAE

Tesserae is the name given to any material that is used in the making of a mosaic. The range is continually expanding: two thousand years ago, the Romans created mosaics from chips of colored stone, while the later Byzantine civilization used shards of colored glass. These days everything from broken china and snail shells, to precious stones—as well as the more traditional tiles—are in common use.

The range of materials available commercially is expanding. Multi-colored mirror tiles are now on sale, along with circular and hexagonal ceramic tiles, to name just a few new developments.

I have concentrated on using materials that are generally available, or have special significance for a particular project. Have fun, though, and remember you can experiment with whatever comes to hand.

Unglazed ceramic tiles

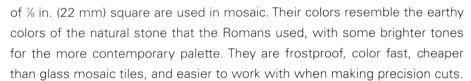

These come in different sizes but usually tiles of ⅞ in. (22 mm) square are used in mosaic. Their colors resemble the earthy colors of the natural stone that the Romans used, with some brighter tones for the more contemporary palette. They are frostproof, color fast, cheaper than glass mosaic tiles, and easier to work with when making precision cuts.

Vitreous glass

These are the most commonly used glass tiles. They come in squares with a beveled, ridged underside. They are both easy to cut and durable, and come in a variety of colors. Originating from Italy, they can be bought loose, or in sheets, and either as single colors, or premixed.

Gemstones and imitations

To really catch someone's eye, add a couple of sparkly stones to your piece. Gemstones are widely available and can be bought flat-backed. Imitation glass gems come foil-backed to add more shine.

Glass nuggets and millefiori

Glass nuggets are wonderful to use in mosaic as they come in a range of colors and sizes. Their flat undersides make adhesion to any base surface simple, and effective. Brightly colored millefiori—made by stretching and cutting long glass rods into hundreds of little disks—are patterned with individual, usually floral designs that really stand out in a mosaic.

Mirror

Mirror also works well in mosaic as it attracts the light and adds sparkle to any piece. Either smash pieces of mirror yourself, or buy ready-cut shapes. Colored mirror tiles are also now very popular, ranging in color from deep orange to cool aquamarine. Be aware of sharp edges when handling them.

Smalti

This Italian glass can be bought either in large pieces, small regular oblongs, or chippings. Their color range is vast and each one is strong and vibrant. The surface is slightly uneven so it will attract and reflect the light. Although more expensive than vitreous glass, mixing smalti in with other tiles works well.

Marble and stone

Marble comes in many colors and can be bought in slabs, regular pieces, or rods. It needs to be cut with either a hammer and hardy, or a wet saw. Stone also comes in a variety of colors and can be found precut or in pebble form. It is very durable, and wonderful for exterior use.

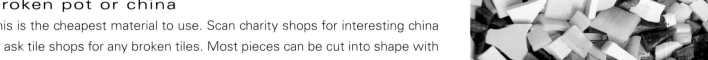

Broken pot or china

This is the cheapest material to use. Scan charity shops for interesting china or ask tile shops for any broken tiles. Most pieces can be cut into shape with tile nippers, or wrapped in wads of newspaper and hit with a hammer.

Natural materials

Nature provides us with a wealth of materials to use in mosaic: fossils that can be bought as well as found in a variety of different shapes and sizes, shells from the beach, or even the shells of snails from your own garden. When varnished, their colors become even more prominent, glowing with a special "wet look".

CUTTING TILES

When you first start cutting mosaic tiles, it is quite common to end up with quite a few misshapen or broken tiles: don't worry, it happens to everybody, and with time and practice your cutting skills will improve. To get the best results when cutting with tile nippers there are a few simple rules to remember:

● Make sure your tile nippers are sharp. The sharper the tool the better the cut; this principle applies to all cutting tools—you'll be amazed at the difference.

● When holding the tile nippers, keep your hands at the bottom of the handles, with the cutting edge turned toward you. You'll find some tiles almost impossible to cut if you hold the nippers too high up the handle. The tool's power relies on leverage, and the higher up the handles you hold the tool, the less cutting power you generate.

● Always cut in a safe manner and be aware of other people around you. When cutting a tile in half or in quarters, always hold the tile with your free hand to give you complete control, stopping any pieces flying off. Never divide tiles by squeezing the nippers with both hands: this can allow slivers of glass or ceramic to fly off in all directions, possibly causing serious injury. Instead, whenever possible, hold both sides of the tile as you cut it. If you are nibbling out a delicate shape and it is impossible to hold both sides of the tile then stand up and make the cut at around knee height—the chippings will fall to the floor, and not fly into your eyes. I often wear protective goggles to minimize any risks when cutting, and I positively insist on this when I am working with children.

To divide a tile in half, position the tile nippers over the center of the tile, with an overlap of about ⅛ in. (3 mm), and cut. If the nippers are positioned more than ¼ in. (6 mm) over the tile, it will be much harder to develop enough controlled energy to cut the tiles cleanly—less is more in this case.

To achieve precision cuts with the ceramic tiles, draw the exact shape you need onto the tile in pencil (the marks will wash away during cleaning). Glass tiles require you to work by eye and may splinter slightly. As you practice, and get a feel for the nippers, start using every edge of the blades to cut different shapes in your tiles.

MIXING SAND AND CEMENT

Sand and cement is widely used in mosaic due to its robust, versatile nature. It is mainly used in its wet state for casting but can also be bought in ready-made slabs, and worked upon directly. For the projects in this book, I have used ready-mixed sand and cement, but they can be equally well bought separately. Sand and cement can also be used as a grout when thinned to create a slurry, which can be gently pressed into the gaps between the tiles. If you are casting with sand and cement and want to grout at a later stage, fill the gaps with dry sand and cast in the usual way. When the mosaic is set, brush the sand out of the gaps and proceed to grout.

1 To make up the sand and cement, either pour the required amount of ready-mixed powder, or 1 part cement to 3 parts sand into a suitable container. Mix them in their dry state until all the particles are evenly distributed within the container. Mix a small amount with an old knife, and a larger quantity with a trowel.

2 To increase the mix's adhesive qualities, add a blob of P.V.A., or wood glue, to the mix along with the required amount of water. If mixing a large quantity, make a well in the center of the mixture, and pour the water in gradually while slowly incorporating more sand and cement from the edges.

3 When enough water has been added to make a thick porridge-like mixture, it is ready for use. If you wish to grout your mosaic with sand and cement, take a little of this mixture and thin it out in a separate container with a little water to create a slurry. Spread a little over the tiles, and gently work it into the gaps between the tiles with your fingers.

DIRECT METHOD

The most common, and simplest, method of creating a mosaic is to stick tesserae directly onto a solid base with an adhesive. This simple technique is identical whatever materials are being used—whether tiles, or smalti, cement-based adhesive, or glue. The most common adhesive used is polyvinyl acetate, commonly referred to as P.V.A., which is water-soluble and ideal for sticking tesserae to wood. Wood glue, in both interior and exterior forms, is a stronger version of P.V.A. Epoxy resin hardens to become incredibly strong, but it can set in a matter of minutes, while cement-based adhesive is perfect for exterior work or when using heavy materials.

1 A cocktail stick, or toothpick, makes an ideal glue dispenser. It holds the ideal amount of adhesive for a small tile, and can be thrown away after use. Never place too many unstuck tiles on the base, they can easily be knocked out of place, ruining hours of hard work. Instead, always stick down the tiles as you go. If you feel at a later stage that you want to change one, simply lever it up from the base.

2 When laying down a row of tiles of a similar cut, it can be time saving to stick down the tiles to a line of glue dispensed onto the base. If working with very small, or delicate pieces, use a cocktail stick to place the glue, giving you excellent control over the flow and reducing the risk of drowning the surrounding tiles. Make sure there is enough adhesive to stick the tiles down firmly but not so much that any excess rises up the tiles' edges as this will later stop the grout filling the gaps adequately.

3 Some surfaces and tesserae require stronger adhesive to bond them together. Cement-based adhesive is incredibly powerful, and its sandy consistency helps hold each tile in place. Depending on your design, it can be applied with a cocktail stick, a palette knife, or a syringe, the last being perfect for creating regular lines of mosaic.

MIXING GROUT

After spending hours creating a mosaic, make time to think about the grout; this is vital to the mosaic's durability, as well as its design. There are many on the market—powdered, pre-prepared, sanded, unsanded, colored, fast- or slow-drying—so it is important that you choose the right one for your mosaic. Always choose a frostproof, waterproof grout for outdoor mosaics. Consider where the piece will be sited, the size of the gaps between the tiles, and the colors of the mosaic. Gray is the traditional color for grout, but for the contemporary piece anything goes. Be sure to choose wisely, though, as the wrong color can ruin a piece. If in doubt, make a test piece to see which color best complements your tiles.

1 Pour the required amount of grout into a suitable container. If you want a lighter gray color, add a little white grout into the bowl and mix them together in their dry state using either an old knife or small trowel until both colors have been fully incorporated into each other.

2 If the grout requires a latex, add that now (not all grouts do, so always read the manufacturer's instructions), before pouring in water slowly until you have a thick creamy mixture. If the grout is too wet, its strength is reduced and it will take longer to dry. If the gaps between the tiles are quite large, make the grout thicker, but if they are narrower, ensure the grout is thinner.

3 To gain a specific shade, mix in a dash of acrylic paint or cement color, and mix well. Remember that the color will be mixed with grout color, reducing its effect—for example, a red acrylic paint mixed into white grout will give a pink grout. Only ever add a little paint: too much can change the properties of the grout, causing cracking and tile staining.

USING GROUT

Like most mosaic techniques, the key to successful grouting is practice. It is, though, a slow technique that needs to be undertaken with care.

Take most care with the timing: don't leave it on the mosaic too long, or it will be impossible to remove from the tiles, but don't clean off too much, too soon,

washing most of the grout away and weakening the piece. The setting time depends on both grout, and surface: any grout on a terracotta pot will dry quickly, while a white grout will dry more slowly than a gray one. Grout usually takes 2 hours to dry completely, but in this time several gentle cleans can take place.

1 First check the width of the gaps on your mosaic: if they exceed ⅛ in. (3 mm) then you will need to use a sanded grout which will increase the durability of the mosaic, and prevent it cracking. Mix the required amount as shown opposite.

2 Use either a squeegee or your hands to spread the grout over your mosaic. Go over the same area several times to ensure the grout has penetrated to the entire depth. Make sure that the most vulnerable tiles around the edge have been surrounded. When all the gaps are filled take off the excess grout and leave for a few minutes.

3 Measure progress by running your finger over a section of grout: if it is still liquid, wait; if it comes away in a powdery form, clean the mosaic with a dry cloth; and if it has begun to set, loosen it up with a damp cloth. Any residue smeared over the tiles from the gaps will be removed by the next clean. Allow the grout to continue drying for a few minutes, and repeat the cleaning with a damp cloth. Again, don't rush: leave the mosaic to sit between cleanings. Let it dry thoroughly and then dust with a dry cloth. Later, clean off any residue on the tiles with hydrochloric acid.

TOOLS

Tile nippers

These can be picked up inexpensively from most good hardware stores, or tile shops. They can cut through most materials that don't exceed a ¼ in. (6 mm) depth. Tile nippers are excellent at precision cutting.

Hammer and hardy

This was the tool of choice from Roman times. It consists of an upturned chisel head embedded into a large chunk of wood, and a hammer. The tiles would be placed onto the chisel head and held while being hit with the hammer. Nowadays, they are mainly used to cut marble, smalti, and stone.

Glass cutter

These cutters have a wheel that scores the glass or mirror tile allowing it to be snapped into the precise shapes required. Cutters with oil reservoirs have increased longevity and are more comfortable to use, while others are designed specifically to cut straight lines, or perfect circles.

Palette knife

Excellent for spreading cement-based adhesive into awkward nooks and crannies, or smoothly over a surface to give an even base for tiles, palette knives are available in a variety of sizes.

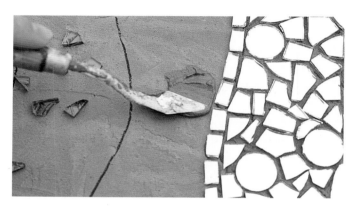

Plastic syringes

These enable glue, or cement-based adhesive to be placed precisely either when a delicate area is being tiled or when the surrounding area needs to be kept clean. They can be obtained from pharmacies and art shops.

Rubber gloves

If a mosaic has very small pieces, it can be safer to grout it by hand, preventing the breakage of any tiles that had not been positioned with enough adhesive. Gloves allow the grout to be worked with ease, stopping your hands drying out, as well as keeping them clean. They are also useful when working with plaster bandage, papier mâché, cement-based adhesive, sand, and cement, and when cutting the sharp edges of aluminum mesh.

Rubber squeegee

These are used to apply grout evenly into the gaps of a mosaic between the tiles, and can be bought in varying sizes. Generally, use a squeegee that is applicable to the size of your mosaic, ensuring that you have complete control over the tool so that it does not dislodge any tiles. Alternatively, if the mosaic is particularly small or delicate, grout by hand.

Marker pens and pencils

When creating a more complicated design, it can be useful to follow a marked outline. Begin with a pencil before covering with a permanent marker which will not smear if the piece needs to be sealed.

Sandpaper

Available in different grades, sandpaper is a useful preparation tool. It works particularly well when smoothing out cement-based adhesive, plaster work, or papier mâché ready for mosaic work.

OTHER TECHNIQUES

Sealing

Most woods and terracotta surfaces are extremely porous, which can affect the strength of adhesives and grouts. Sealing the surface of the base beforehand with a solution of 1 part P.V.A., or wood glue, to 3 parts water will ensure that tiles stick firmly, and your mosaic remains stronger for longer.

Scoring

If working on a smooth surface such as MDF (medium density fiberboard) it is always preferable to score, or "key", the surface to create some grip for tiles that have a tendency to slip out of place. Using a craft knife, score the surface in both directions to give a diamond-shaped effect. Do this after any design has been drawn onto the base, but before the wood has been sealed.

Staining or varnishing

When working on exterior-grade wood for an outside piece, always protect every surface against the elements. Most tiles are frostproof, and the grout waterproof, leaving the bottom and sides to protect. Wood stains come in a variety of colors and can be painted on with a brush; 2 to 3 coats are advisable. Varnishes also come in different types, such as matt or gloss, and are applied in the same way.

Sealants

To protect a mosaic further from both water and frost damage, sealants can be applied after the work is complete. Stone mosaics, especially, look particularly attractive when sealed as it gives them a shiny "wet look". Some sealants can be brushed over the whole mosaic while others need to be painted directly onto the grout—always check the instructions of the individual sealant before use.

INDIRECT OR REVERSE METHOD

This method allows portable pieces of mosaic to be made that can either be installed into a wall, ceiling, or floor, or cast into sand and cement. It also allows for pieces to be made in a studio before being installed in your chosen spot. If the mosaic is large, it can then be divided into smaller pieces with a craft knife, with a record kept of the position of each piece in the design. Another advantage of this method is that it enables you to use different tiles of varying depths which, when cast or assembled will create a smooth, even surface.

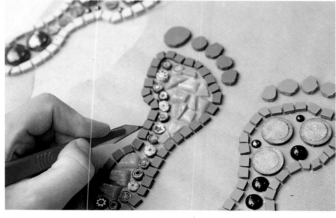

1 Draw the initial design with pencil onto brown parcel paper that has been secured to a flat surface. Stick down your tiles using water-soluble adhesive—gum arabic is excellent for this, or P.V.A. diluted with an equal amount of water. Make sure that all tiles are placed face down, and scraggy edges are facing toward you. When all tiles have been glued into place allow them to dry and then use a craft knife to cut out the design.

2 If the mosaic is going to be secured to a wall, apply a thin layer of cement-based adhesive to the designated area. To bind the tiles together, "butter" either cement-based adhesive or waterproof grout into the gaps of the mosaic, depending on your preference, allowing a little to rest on top to ensure bonding. Secure the mosaic to the wall, smoothing out any lumps and allow it to dry for 24 hours.

3 When the mosaic has set, wash over the top of the brown paper with a sponge soaked in warm water to loosen the glue, and then gently peel the paper away from the tiles. Finally, clean any remaining adhesive from the surface of the tiles, and regrout to cover any airholes.

POTS AND PLANTERS

ivy-leaf hanging pot

We have the most wonderful vine-covered wall at the end of our garden, and this was the true source of inspiration for this mosaic. I love the subtle greens of the tumbling leaves; and, to capture the subtlety of the natural tones, I chose three key shades for the leaves, then matched them to the colors for the stems. Finally, I used a pale background that helps to make the leaves stand out. When working out a color scheme, it can be rewarding to look closely at the source of your own inspiration, particularly in the garden: flowers and plants offer wonderful arrangements to copy.

you will need:

Frostproof, terracotta, flat-backed wall pot (approx 9in. [23cm] high by 8in. [20cm] across)

Ceramic and glass tiles: 20 green glass; 20 gold glass; 6 gold leaf; 75 off-white and light yellow ceramic

Pencil and water-resistant pen

Tile nippers

P.V.A.

Cement-based adhesive

Frostproof waterproof grout

1 Transfer your design using the template on page 123 onto the pot with the pencil. Go over the outline with the water-resistant pen.

2 Seal the pot inside and out with a mixture of 1 part P.V.A. to 3 parts water, and allow to dry. This forms a protective layer between the pot and the adhesive, adding further strength and protection from the elements.

3 Use the tile nippers to shape the tiles and then stick them down with a cement-based adhesive. As well as being an incredibly strong exterior adhesive, this also holds your tiles in place when working on a curved structure. Allow the adhesive to dry thoroughly before you begin the grouting.

4 Using a frostproof grout mixed according to the instructions, rub the mixture into all the gaps between the mosaics going over the same place several times to ensure that all gaps have been filled. Remove the excess and leave for about ten minutes until you can see it start to dry. I would advise wearing rubber gloves at this point because grout dries out the skin.

5 Remove the grout by cleaning off the excess with a dry cloth. Leave to dry for around ten minutes, then wipe again with a wet cloth. Leave to dry completely, then polish the pot with a clean dry cloth to remove any dust.

ALTERNATIVES

Mosaic pots are a great way to add a season-round splash of color to small corners of the garden that may need extra interest. Just by adding one or two vibrantly-colored mosaic pots to an ordinary collection of pots you can add instant chic to a planting arrangement. Above, I used a very simple grid pattern which required no tile cutting. The daisy motif pot (right) was slightly more complicated but very effective.

recycled concrete planter

A friend recently moved into a new house and inherited a lot of the former occupant's rubbish. One of the pieces ready for throwing out was a worn slab of concrete with eight hollow sections. Instead, to become an ideal planter, it just needed tidying up—and mosaic was the perfect medium. Keep a sharp eye out for other bases for mosaics—what is deemed one person's rubbish can definitely become another's treasure.

you will need:

Concrete slab

100 glass brown or gold tiles

200 assorted beige and pale pink ceramic tiles

P.V.A

Exterior-grade wood glue

Cement-based adhesive

Tile nippers

Waterproof grout

1 Clean off any dirt from the surface of the piece and seal with 1 part P.V.A. to 3 parts water. Allow to dry.

2 Cut the glass tiles into quarters, leaving 3 intact. Cut 70 ceramic tiles into quarters, 70 into 16ths and leave the rest whole.

3 Using an exterior-grade wood glue, stick down glass quarters around the top edge of each opening and 3 whole glass tiles equally down the center of the planter. Fix whole and quartered ceramic tiles around the edge of the whole piece.

4 Fill in the rest of the top with rows of ceramic 16ths. For the sides, use a cement-based adhesive as this will stop the tiles from slipping. Place a row of whole ceramic tiles around the base, followed by a row of glass quarters, and finally a row of ceramic quarters. Allow the adhesives to dry completely before using a waterproof grout in the usual way.

two-handled urn

Unglazed ceramic urns, pots and jugs can be picked up very cheaply from any garden center, in a huge variety of shapes and sizes. They look wonderful as they are but, personally, I think they are crying out to be decorated with mosaic tiles! The scheme I've used is a delicate mixture of five unglazed ceramic colors, nibbled into a variety of shapes. I've specifically used ceramic as these tiles are easy to cut into precise shapes but, if you want to achieve a brighter effect, do feel free to substitute the ceramic tiles for glass.

you will need:

Unglazed ceramic urn, 14in. (36cm) high

Approx. 45 tiles in each of 5 different colors

P.V.A.

Tile nippers

1in. (2.5cm) paintbrush

Cement-based adhesive

Waterproof grout

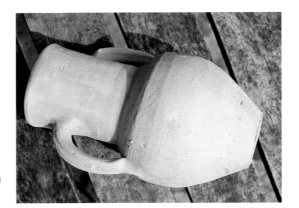

1 Choose your urn – you can use a secondhand piece and wash it and leave it to dry before you start. Rest it on a wooden or softer surface as you work.

2 Using a soft paintbrush, seal the surface using a solution of 1 part P.V.A. to 3 parts water and allow to dry.

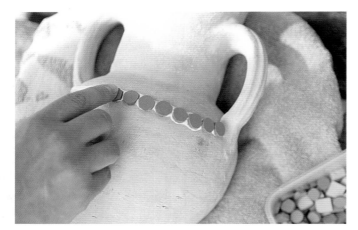

3 Cut all your tiles into quarters. Depending on your own preference, divide some of the quarters further—into circles, in half, or in quarter again. Use a cement-based adhesive to prepare the position of the first row of tiles.

4 Place a row of tiles around the line of adhesive, ensuring that the line remains parallel to the base of the urn. Work on one side of the urn first, before repeating the design on the reverse.

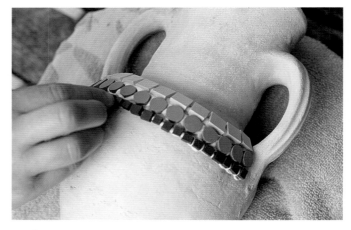

5 Continue adding rings of tiles, down to the base of the urn and then right up to the lip using different shapes and colors for each row, before sealing the mosaic with waterproof grout in the usual way (see pages 14–15).

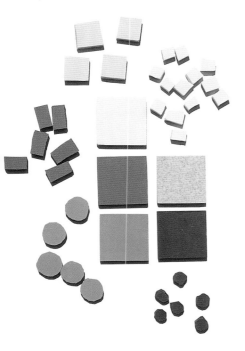

TIPS

● To keep the urn in a stable position while you are working, rest it on a soft surface or an old towel. This will also protect the tiles on the underside of the urn from coming into contact with a hard surface that could be damaging.

● If you want to use another color scheme, start off with a handful of colors and play around with different combinations until you find the one that works for you.

● Using a single color can also create a dramatic effect, if teamed with a contrasting grout.

cone planter

A while ago, I bought some scented patio torches to brighten up summer evenings in the garden. They were suspended from metal rods stuck into the ground, but, after using the candles, I was left with two defunct rods until it occurred to me that they would make ideal holders for cone-shaped mosaics. What you then put in them is up to you: they are perfect candle holders, as well as planters or, for an alternative effect, they could be filled with shiny glass nuggets.

you will need:

Aluminum mesh or chicken wire,
10 x 18in. (25 x 46cm)

100 assorted glass tiles

Masking tape

Plaster bandage

Plant sprayer

Palette knife

Sandpaper

Tile nippers

Cement-based adhesive

Waterproof grout

1 Mold the mesh or chicken wire into a cone shape and secure it in place with masking tape.

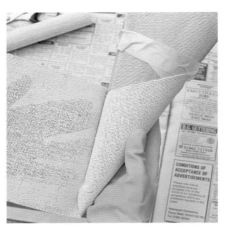

2 Cut the plaster bandage into 10in. (25cm) strips. Wrap them around the cone while still dry.

3 Spray water over the bandage and smooth out the plaster by hand.

4 Repeat until the entire exterior of the cone is covered, as well as the inner lip. Allow to dry.

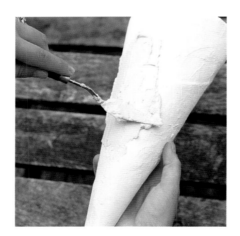

5 When the plaster is completely set, apply a thin but even layer of cement-based adhesive over both the outer cone, and the inner surface, with a palette knife.

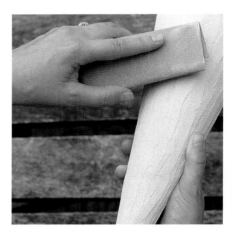

6 When this has dried, sand off any lumpy bits until you have a smooth surface on which to add your mosaic.

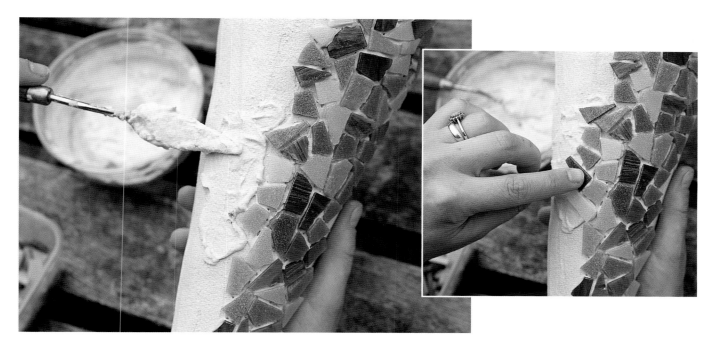

7 Cut the glass tiles into random pieces and fix to the cone with cement-based adhesive. Leave a small gap between each tile, making sure there is enough adhesive to embed the tile in, but not so much that it rises over the top of each tile. Cover the entire outside of the cone and the inner lip. Allow to dry. Finish by sealing the mosaic with a waterproof grout. Allow to dry, before suspending the cone from the metal rod that has been secured firmly into the ground.

TIP

If you decide to use the mosaic cones as plant holders, repot your chosen plant into a small plastic tumbler, and carefully place it inside the cone. These beakers are usually longer, and thinner than plant pots, and should fit inside your cones more easily.

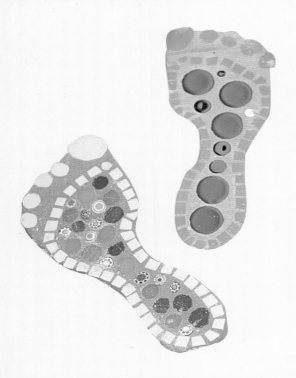

GARDEN ADDITIONS

fountain

When I saw this preprepared fountain in the garden center, I just had to have it! Not only was it made of real stone but it also had a perfectly flat top—ideal to work mosaic on—and was made up of a variety of colors, ranging all the way from sharp, crystal whites to the deepest granite blacks: all of which were colors I could replicate in glass tiles. I used mirror in the design to accentuate the flow of the water, and add more sparkle to the finished piece. Any manufactured fountain can be used, as long as it has a relatively smooth surface.

you will need:

Smooth-topped, stone fountain, approximately 18 x 9in. (46 x 23cm)

32 black glass tiles

34 gray glass tiles

32 small mirror tiles

40 white glass tiles

P.V.A

Tile nippers

Cement-based adhesive

Masking tape

Waterproof grout

1 When you have chosen your fountain, seal the area of the stone that is going to be worked on with a mixture of 1 part P.V.A. to 3 parts water, and allow to dry.

2 Cut the black, gray, and half of the white tiles into quarters. Cut the remaining white tiles into random-shaped pieces. Cut all but 3 of your mirror tiles in half, the rest into quarters.

3 Using cement-based adhesive, arrange the quartered colored and halved mirror tiles in rows of each color around the water spout, mirroring the natural patterns of the rock. Work inward until all the even-shaped tiles have been used.

4 Around the edge of the spout, stick down the quartered mirror tiles, and fill in the central area with the random-shaped white tiles. Allow to dry overnight.

5 To keep the rest of the stone clean, and achieve a sharp grout edge, place small, protective strips of masking tape around the outside of the tiles all around the design.

6 Cover the stone with waterproof grout, ensuring every space is filled and watertight. Clean off when dry and set up the water supply.

children's footprints

With the popularity of casting a child's foot in bronze as a reminder of their early years, I began to think of ways of recording a child's growth in mosaic. Here, I replicated my daughter's footprints using mosaic, sand, and cement, creating a patchwork of individual prints for her own sand garden. Make as many as you like—a single pair, a pathway walking across a lawn, or even prints that grow in size with your child.

for each foot you will need:

7 ceramic tiles

Collection of flat-backed beads, glass nuggets, circular glass or ceramic tiles

Poster paint

Brown paper

Tracing paper

Pencil

Board

Parcel paper

Tape

Tile nippers

Gum arabic

Craft knife

Plasticine

Petroleum jelly

Paintbrush

2 bowls for mixing sand and cement

1 cup of premixed sand and cement

P.V.A.

Plastic wrap

Scourer

Sealable bag

Waterproof grout

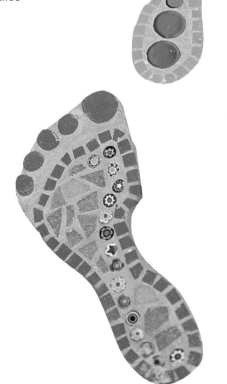

HOW TO MAKE YOUR CHILD'S FOOTPRINT

Cover the sole of your child's foot with poster paint and let them walk across a sheet of plain paper, making footprints. When the paint has dried make a tracing of the best print. Alternatively, use the template provided on page 122.

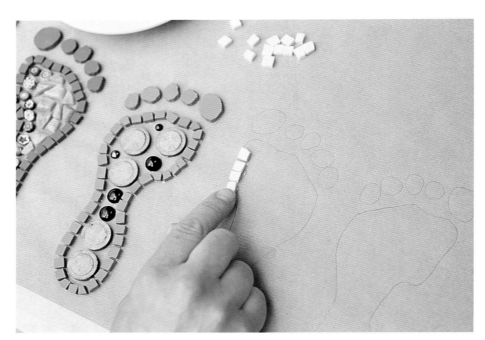

1 Cover a board with brown parcel paper, taping down the sides, and transfer the tracing onto the paper, turning the tracing paper over to make a mirror image for the other foot. Repeat this as many times as you require. Cut ceramic tiles into the shape of toes, following a pencil guide drawn onto each one, and cut the rest of the tiles into 16ths. Stick the toes down with the gum, and outline the foot with the tiny mosaic squares. The center of the foot is yours to have fun with, fill it with as many different tiles or objects as you like. Remember that differences in height will not matter as you are working in reverse.

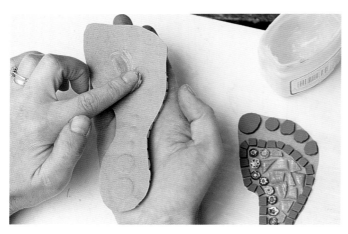

2 After cutting around the foot with a craft knife, lift the print away and place it onto the casting board, rubbing a small amount of petroleum jelly across its underside to secure it in place.

3 Mold Plasticine into a sausage shape, and then roll out a long strip around 3in. (7cm) high. Place this around the foot, pressing down the edges to form a secure bond with the board. Gently press the end pieces together so the foot is completely surrounded by a wall of Plasticine. With a brush, paint petroleum jelly around the inside of the Plasticine to act as a release agent.

4 In a bowl, mix up the sand and cement with a little P.V.A. and water until you have a thick liquid with the consistency of heavy cream. Remove a little bit of this into another bowl and thin it down further with water to create a slurry. Gently pour the slurry over the foot, pressing it firmly into the gaps.

5 Add the rest of the sand and cement mixture, smoothing the surface. Gently tap the board for a while: the vibrations will release most of the air bubbles in the mixture, ensuring a solid casting.

6 To ensure that the sand and cement set firm, create an airtight covering around the Plasticine mold with plastic wrap, leaving the foot on a level surface to harden. The plastic wrap will hold in moisture, allowing the sand and cement to dry out extremely slowly. Leave to dry for 4–5 days.

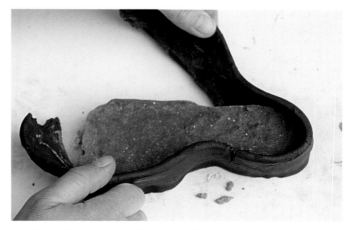

7 After this time, carefully remove the plastic wrap covering and free the foot from the Plasticine mold by gently easing it away from the sides of the foot. Put the used Plasticine into a sealable bag as this can be used again.

8 Turn the foot over and gently remove the brown paper on which the tiles were originally placed, leaving a mirror image of the design.

9 The sand and cement is by no means fully set at this stage but the foot will be strong enough for you to clean carefully any stray mixture off the tops of the tiles using a scourer. Place the foot into a resealable bag and allow to dry out very slowly. If it dries too fast it will crack—two weeks is a good length of time to allow.

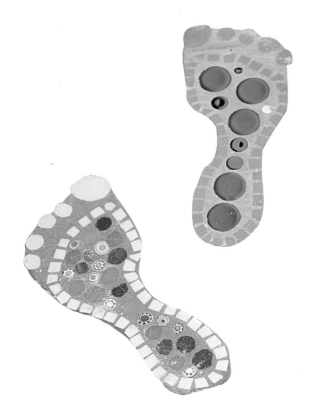

10 After two weeks, remove the foot from the bag and let it dry out completely in a shady place. If any air holes are visible, grout over the surface and clean in the usual way, bearing in mind that the grout will dry a lot quicker than usual as its depth is minimal.

house number

All buildings require a name or number to identify them, usually in the form of a little plaque. As mosaic is one of the most durable art forms, it makes for an ideal project for an exterior setting. Practical as well as decorative, it will catch the eye of all those who need to find it! I have created a design based around tulips but perhaps you could incorporate the plant or animal with most relevance to you.

you will need:

Plywood square, 9 x 9in.
(23 x 23cm)

52 black ceramic tiles

70 off-white ceramic tiles

5 white ceramic tiles

12 assorted purple glass or
mirror tiles

6 assorted red and orange
glass or mirror tiles

15 green glass or mirror tiles

Pencil

Permanent marker

P.V.A.

Tile nippers

Exterior-grade wood glue

Waterproof grout

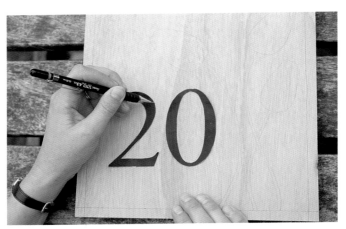

1 Using the template provided (see pages 124–125), draw out the design for your house number in pencil, then, when you are happy with the positioning of the numbers, go over it with the permanent marker.

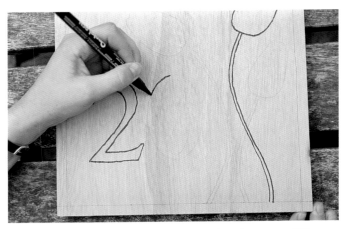

2 Repeat the process with the tulip template (see page 127). Seal the wood by painting over the surface with a mixture of 1 part P.V.A. to 3 parts water. Allow to dry.

3 Cut 40 of the black tiles into quarters and stick them around the outer edge and sides of the plywood square with wood glue, leaving gaps between each one. To achieve the exact shape you require for the numbers, draw the cutting lines onto your tiles with a pencil, making the angles as regular as possible. Cut the glass tiles for the tulip design into very small pieces, down to ⅛in. (3 mm) square—though they can be slightly larger.

4 Starting with a ring of tiles around the outside of the flower, continue to the center of each tulip. Cut the green tiles into regular rectangles and glue them along the stalk.

5 Cut the white and off-white tiles into 16ths. Lay them down as evenly as possible around the outside edges of the tulips and numbers, shaping where necessary, until every detail has a background color edge. Fill in the rest of the background with horizontal lines of white tiles. Allow to dry.

6 Finish off the mosaic by sealing with a waterproof grout in the usual way (see pages 14–15).

VARIATION

The architectural style of your home may dictate the design of your mosaic. Here, an Art Deco style has been used with vibrant, contrasting colors to make up a strong, linear design. To add to the piece's clarity, a black grout highlights each tile and gives the plaque a sharp finish.

birdbath

I found this little birdbath in a flower shop and, as pretty as it was in its own right, I knew I could create something a little more eye-catching and individual. When hanging outside my window, with its tiles sparkling in the sun, it would be the perfect invitation to the local songbirds! Because of the vivid colors of the tiles, I deliberately created a simple design that would allow the mosaic to shine.

you will need:

Metal-framed birdbath

130 assorted blue glass tiles

20 silver leaf tiles

7 gold leaf tiles

Marker pen

Circular mirror
(approx. 6in. [15cm] wide)

Cement-based adhesive

Waterproof grout

Tile nippers

Toothbrush

1 Draw a circular design onto the base of the birdbath twice the diameter than the mirror you will use.

2 Cut all but 6 of the blue glass tiles into quarters, dividing the remainder into small random shapes. Cut all the silver tiles into quarters and cut 50 of those in half again. Cut all the gold tiles in quarters and cut 10 of those into quarters again. Using cement-based adhesive, start by fixing down a square of blue tiles around the edge. Then place the silver quarters around the outside of the circle. Next, turn some of the silver halves upside down—they should be a vivid blue color—and run them around the inside of your first circle. The next row consists of the gold 16ths. As you approach the very middle, place the mirror in the exact center and fill in the gap with the random blue glass. Allow to dry.

3 To fix tiles along the vertical arms of the birdbath, tilt it until it is in a good position to work from, and run blue tiles along the entire length of each arm and on the inside of the bath itself, adding the occasional gold tile and a final row of silver halves. Let each side dry completely before you start work on the other sides. Grout in the usual way (see pages 14–15), using a toothbrush to clean any hard-to-reach nooks and crannies.

summertime sphere

This project is perfect for using up all the misshapen and left-over tiles you may have saved from previous projects. Mix these fragments with some smalti, beads, shells, mirror or anything else that comes to hand to create a vibrant, stunning garden sphere. Another bonus for many is that no grouting is required! The vivid colors of this sphere enable it to be placed either alone as a feature, or semi-hidden within a planted border to add a little excitement.

you will need:

Unglazed ceramic sphere

Left-over tiles, smalti, shells, beads, mirror fragments, fossils, and broken tiles in various sizes

Permanent marker

P.V.A.

Cement-based adhesive

Towel

1 With a permanent marker, draw your design onto a ceramic sphere. Here, I have included long blades of grass interwoven through an abstract design.

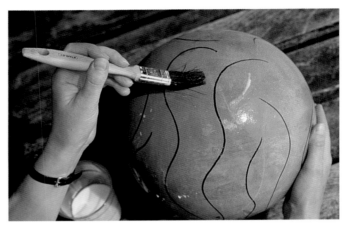

2 To prepare for tiling, seal the sphere using 1 part P.V.A. to 3 parts water, and allow to dry.

3 Using cement-based adhesive, start embedding your tiles. As the design requires no grouting try to place the tiles as close to each other as possible so the adhesive is mostly hidden, breaking up any blank areas with a few small beads.

4 Make sure that you have applied enough adhesive to hold your tiles as there will be no extra help from the grout, and try to cover all the surface of the sphere: any patches of ceramic showing through will look untidy and unfinished.

5 To work on the sides, lay the sphere down on a towel, allowing the ball to rest at the required angle while protecting any delicate pieces from a hard surface. When finished, allow the adhesive to dry overnight before placing the sphere in your garden.

VARIATION

This sphere was inspired by the rich colors of a country garden in high summer but it would look equally stunning with another season's color palette—the russets, golds, and deep reds of Fall, or the crisp whites and silver with streaks of icy blue for a wintry feel. Spring, of course would require fresh greens and clear blues, with hints of brighter colors to depict the appearance of seasonal flowers. Other variants include less abstract alternatives that include a motif, like this fish, with its own particular relevance. Perhaps it could be replaced with a special plant, or even a date commemorating an anniversary.

suncatcher

To add some extra sparkle, hang a couple of these suncatchers in a tree and watch the reflective light bounce around your garden as the sun moves from the strength of midday to the glow of the evening. Quick and easy to assemble, they make an ideal project for the budding mosaicist. Make more of a feature of the hanging line by drilling holes into small shells and threading them alongside the suncatchers and beads. Alternatively, hang several on top of each other in a vertical row by drilling holes in the bottom, as well as the top, of each piece of plywood, looping beaded nylon thread between the suncatchers. These could either be color co-ordinated, or personalized by every member of the family.

you will need:

Sheet of exterior-grade plywood, 2 x 7in. (5 x 18cm)

14 large mirror tiles

14 assorted glass blue tiles

P.V.A.

Tile nippers

Exterior wood glue

Waterproof grout

Assorted beads

Nylon thread

1 Cut your exterior grade wood to size and drill a hole ½in. (1cm) from the top.

2 Cut the tiles into randomly shaped pieces and stick them to the wood using wood glue, leaving suitable gaps for grout around each tile.

3 When both sides of the light catcher have been covered with tiles, leave them to dry completely.

4 Using a waterproof grout, carefully cover all the gaps—while avoiding blocking up the hole drilled earlier—and when dry, clean off any excess grout. Thread some beads onto a piece of nylon string and pass this through the hole before tying it in a loop and hanging the suncatcher in the garden.

ammonite
stepping stone

This piece was inspired by the wonderful spirals and aged soft colors of an ammonite fossil. Ideal as a match for projects and pieces already established in the garden, the stone works best in a subtle range of natural shades; here, the fossil stone is placed by a butterfly stepping stone that has already aged beautifully—a characteristic of mosaics that make them ideally suited to outdoor use. In contrast to the subtle hues of these stones, I also created a smaller, purely ornamental stone to go in a tub I had planted with a range of pink alpine plants. This stone is quite jewel-like in quality with mirror tiles and bright, reflective ceramic tiles, adding light and interest to a small corner of the garden.

you will need:

Brown paper
(approx. 12in. x 12in. [30 x 30cm])

Ceramic tiles: 60 brown;
20 dark brown; 30 black; 20 off-white

Pencil

Masking tape

Backing board (1in.[2.5cm] to larger in size all round than brown paper)

Tile nippers

Palette knife

Glue stick or P.V.A. glue and water, mixed in a 50:50 ratio

Scissors or craft knife

Plastic bowl (approx 13in. [33cm] in diameter)

Petroleum jelly

Bucket or large bowl

Bag of mixed sand and cement

Chicken wire

Plastic wrap

1 Carefully secure the piece of brown paper onto the backing board using the masking tape. Draw the ammonite onto brown paper using the template provided on pages 118–119. Copy the shape you want to make on the tile by drawing in pencil on to one side.

2 Using the tile nippers, nibble each tile into shape, rather than trying to cut large chunks at a time.

3 Dilute the P.V.A. to one part glue to one part water, or use the gum stick to dab a small amount of glue on to each tile, and stick down onto the brown paper according to your design. Remember to put the glue on the pencil-free side as this is the side that will show.

4 When you have completed your mosaic, cut out the design using the craft knife or scissors.

5 Take the plastic bowl and grease the whole of the inside with the petroleum jelly. This will act as a release agent when you come to turn out your cement stepping stone. Lay the mosaic, paper side down, into the bowl and press down to secure it in place.

6 Mix your cement and a small amount of slurry (see page 12). Gently place the slurry on to the mosaic with a palette knife and push it into all the gaps between the mosaics.

7 Then add half of your sand and cement mix to the bowl and spread over the slurry mix. Place the chicken wire on the top to reinforce your stepping stone. Add the rest of the sand and cement and gently rock the bowl until the surface is smooth.

8 Cover the whole bowl with plastic wrap to keep in the moisture so that the sand and cement mix dries very slowly. Tap the sides of the bowl to remove any air bubbles that can occur during the drying process. Leave for 4–5 days.

9 After a few days you can uncover the mosaic and tip it out of the bowl.

10 Remove the brown paper and scrub off any sand and cement that has overlapped any of the tiles. Then put the stepping stone back into the bowl and re-cover with the plastic wrap. Leave two weeks for it to dry out completely. If there are any air holes or unfilled gaps, you can regrout these areas with some of the sand and cement mix.

ORNAMENTAL STONE

This much smaller piece, created to sparkle, is made purely for decoration. The mirror tiles and glass tiles I have used here would not be suitable for a stepping stone as they are not as durable as ceramic tiles. A dyed black cement is used here to create a dramatic contrast to the brightly colored tiles.

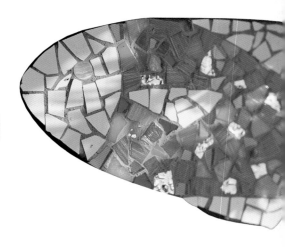

shoal of fish

This is a wonderful project—whether your garden contains a pond or not! Fish have the most amazing range of colors, shapes, sizes, and patterns, so really anything goes when you are including them in mosaic designs. These fish are embedded into sand and cement and are very strong and durable. They can either lie semi-submerged in a pond or cast into a sand and cement border. Alternatively, they would make excellent planters if the gaps between the fish were to be filled in with little alpine plants.

for each fish you will need:

Board

Brown paper

Approx. 40 assorted tiles and imitation gemstones

Masking tape

Pencil

Tile nippers

Gum arabic

Craft knife

Surface for casting

Petroleum jelly

Plasticine

2 cups ready-mixed sand and cement

2 bowls for mixing sand and cement

P.V.A.

Plastic wrap

Large sealable bag

Scourer

Waterproof grout

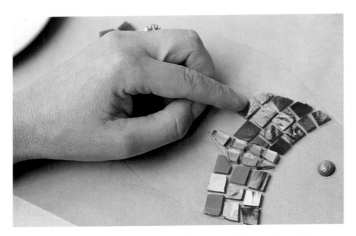

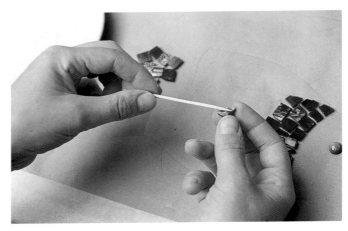

1 Cover a board with brown parcel paper and tape down the sides. Draw around the template provided on page 121 to create the outline of a fish, and fill in the center with a design of your choice.

2 Depending on the design, cut up your tiles into squares, specific shapes or random pieces and stick down with gum. Remember that you are working in reverse so the front of each tile must be stuck to the paper.

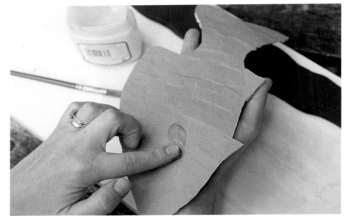

3 Continue until the whole fish is covered in your chosen tesserae, making sure to leave adequate gaps between each tile. Put aside and allow the gum to dry completely before continuing.

4 Cut out the fish with a craft knife, keeping close to the edge of the design. Handling with care, put a few blobs of petroleum jelly onto the paper side of the fish and, pressing down firmly, secure to the casting surface.

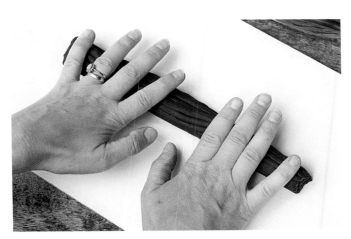

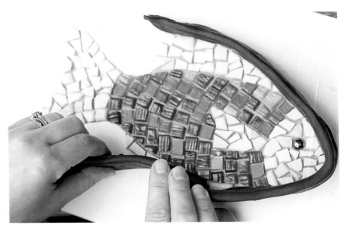

5 Roll out the Plasticine into a sausage and then flatten it until you have a strip that is around 2in. (5cm) high, and long enough to go all the way around the fish.

6 Keeping close to the fish's edge, carefully wrap the strip of Plasticine around the body of the fish, securing the end pieces together, and making sure the bottom of the strip is fully bonded with the surface of the board.

7 Mix up the sand and cement in a bowl, adding water very slowly until it resembles extra thick cream. To increase the adhesive qualities of the sand and cement, add a large blob of P.V.A. glue and mix in well.

8 Remove a small amount into another bowl, adding a little more water to create a slurry. This needs to be a fairly thin solution as it needs to fit easily into the gaps between the tiles in the same way as grout if it is to form a solid base for the mosaic.

9 Carefully pour this over the fish and ease it into the gaps using your fingers. Add the rest of the sand and cement and smooth the surface.

10 Tap the side of the board for a while to release the air pockets and then wrap the fish completely with plastic wrap, taping down the edges. Leave to dry on a flat surface.

11 After around three days, the fish can be very carefully unwrapped, and the Plasticine removed. Try to be very delicate at this stage as the fish is very fragile. Place the Plasticine into a sealable bag so that it can be used again.

12 Gently peel the paper away from the tiles. It should still be damp enough to be eased gently off the tiles, but if some areas stick, just add a little hot water to the reverse of the paper, leave for a few minutes, and remove.

13 Using a scourer, remove any unwanted residue of sand and cement from the tops of the tiles – it is still soft enough to do this easily but, left for another week, it would be much harder. Be as gentle as possible at this stage – the fish's tail is a weak spot. If the worst should happen and the tail breaks do not worry: let them both dry out in the usual way and then glue them together. Grout will cover any cracks and no one will be the wiser.

14 Place the fish in a large, sealable bag and allow it to dry slowly over the next couple of weeks. Remove it from the bag and place the fish in a cool shady place to dry out completely for another week. Even at this stage, if you were to put it in full sunshine, there is a large chance it would crack. If you feel the fish needs grouting (and it may not), grout in the usual way, bearing in mind that the process will be a lot quicker due to the shallowness of the grout.

sparkling fish

This sparkling fish started life many years ago as a simple papier-mâché structure made out of chicken wire. Over the years, as his color began to fade, he began to look less and less attractive, so I decided to bejewel him in glassy mosaic tiles, mirror pieces and imitation gemstones. Now he has been given new life that will stand the test of time, and he now withstands all the elements can throw at him. Place the fish next to a pond to allow the water to reflect over his body to create even greater shine and radiance.

you will need:

2 sections of aluminum mesh, or chicken wire, 24 x 24in. (61 x 61 cm)

9oz. (250g) of 4 different colored glass mosaic tiles

35oz. (1000g) of assorted mirror tiles

Assortment of foil-backed cabouchons, or imitation gemstones

2 glass nuggets

Fuse wire

2 rolls of plaster bandage cement-based adhesive

Sandpaper

P.V.A. and paintbrush

Marker pen

2 x 1in. (2.5 cm) washers

Epoxy glue

Tile nippers

Palette knife

Waterproof grout

1 Create a frame for the fish's body from by molding one section of aluminum mesh or chicken wire into a cigar shape around scrunched-up newspaper. Shape the head into a point and secure the opening with fuse wire.

2 Cut out the shapes for 4 fins and the tail from the second sheet of wire mesh.

3 Position the fins and tail onto the body with masking tape before fixing them in place with fuse wire. Remember that the fish will be supported by the bottom three fins so they need to be evenly placed.

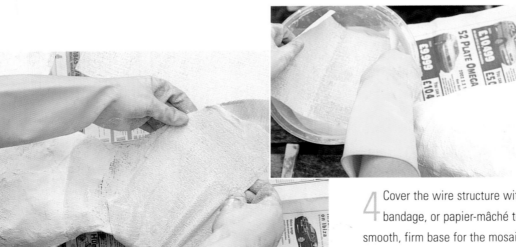

4 Cover the wire structure with a few layers of either plaster bandage, or papier-mâché to give added strength and create a smooth, firm base for the mosaic work.

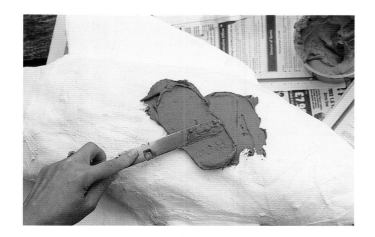

5 When the bandage has dried, apply a ⅛in.- (3-mm-) thick layer of cement-based adhesive over the entire fish with a palette knife. Cover one side, allowing time to dry, before turning the fish around to complete. To achieve a smooth finish, dip your palette knife in warm water and gently run it up and down the area you have been working on. When the whole fish has been covered, allow it to dry and smooth off any lumps and bumps with sandpaper. Draw your design onto the fish using a permanent marker and then seal with a mixture of 3 parts water to 1 part P.V.A, using a paintbrush. One coat is all you need.

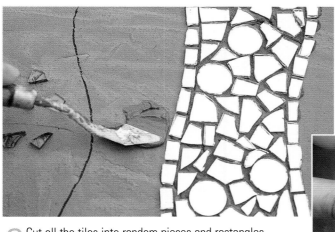

6 Cut all the tiles into random pieces and rectangles. Make the fish's eyes by sticking the glass nuggets onto the washers with epoxy glue. Using cement-based adhesive, lay down your tiles leaving an ⅛-in.- (3 mm-) gap between each one for the grout. Work on one side of the fish at a time, and allow to dry before grouting in the usual way.

TIP

To achieve the best shine, grout in the usual way, gently massaging the mixture into all the nooks and crannies. Immediately remove any excess, and allow to dry for a few minutes, then clean with a dry cloth before carefully wiping with a damp cloth. When completely dry, dust the fish with a dry cloth to bring up the sparkle.

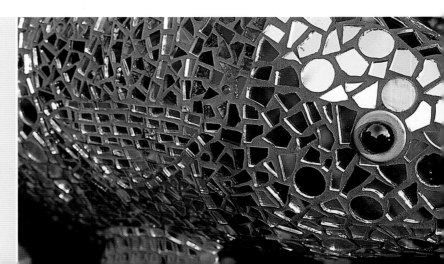

ivy vine

you will need:

10 squares of aluminum mesh

90 assorted green and gold mirror or glass tiles

Fuse wire

Cement-based adhesive

Palette knife

Sandpaper

Marker pen and pencil

Tile nippers

White grout

Green acrylic paint

Gold contour paint

Garden wire

I'm very attracted to ivy and this project accentuates everything I love about the plant: its variety of colors, and its draping nature, the shape of the leaves, and its ability to blend in with other plants. What I don't like is the plant's ability to grow everywhere it shouldn't, so there is the added bonus that you can hang this stunning garland anywhere without the fear that it will start to spread!

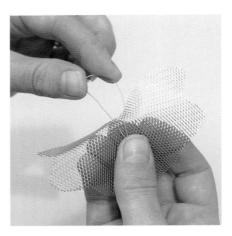

1 Fold each square of mesh in half and cut out the shape of half an ivy leaf, or keep the squares unfolded and transfer the templates on page 123. If you use your own design, either draw it onto the mesh with a marker pen or cut the leaves out by eye.

2 Open up, and secure a small loop of fuse wire into the back of each leaf. Twist the ends of the wire to secure and cut off any excess.

3 Holding onto the wire loop, gently spread a layer of cement-based adhesive over the leaf with a palette knife, making sure it penetrates the holes of the mesh. Turn the leaf over and smooth out the back adding more adhesive if needed. Allow to dry before smoothing off any lumps with sandpaper.

4 Draw on the veins of the leaf in pencil. Cut the mirror or glass tiles into small, random pieces with tile nippers, ready for use.

5 Working on one section of the leaf at a time, spread a small amount of cement-based adhesive between the ivy veins and lay down your tiles, making sure the adhesive doesn't rise above them.

6 Remember to leave small gaps between each tile and a slightly larger gap along the veins. Allow to dry when finished.

7 Mix a small amount of green acrylic paint to the white grout, adding more until you have reached your desired shade of green.

8 Grout in the usual way (see pages 14–15), but also spread a thin layer of grout over the back of each leaf as well.

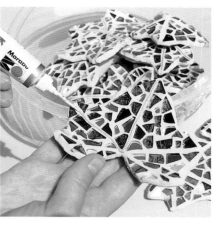

9 Using gold contour paint, draw in the veins of just a few of your leaves to add some extra sparkle, and allow to dry.

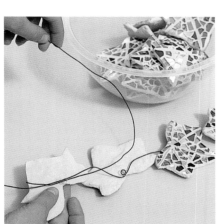

10 Cut a length of green garden wire and thread it though each of the leaves, securing each one in place with a loop of wire.

butterfly on a stone

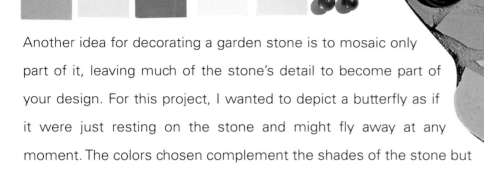

Another idea for decorating a garden stone is to mosaic only part of it, leaving much of the stone's detail to become part of your design. For this project, I wanted to depict a butterfly as if it were just resting on the stone and might fly away at any moment. The colors chosen complement the shades of the stone but they could be changed to match your favorite butterfly.

you will need:

1 garden stone

4 dark blue ceramic tiles

1 light blue ceramic tile

1 black ceramic tile

2 light green tiles

1 light yellow tile

4 imitation gemstones

Pencil

Permanent marker

P.V.A.

Tile nippers

Cement-based adhesive

Epoxy glue

Cocktail stick

Masking tape

Waterproof grout

Toothbrush

1 Using the template provided on page 120, draw around the butterfly—first in pencil, filling in the middle detail, and then with a permanent marker.

2 With a solution of 1 part P.V.A. to 3 parts water, seal the area of the stone that you are going to work on. Allow to dry.

3 Draw cutting lines directly onto the tiles in pencil to allow you to split them to the precise shape of the butterfly with the tile nippers.

4 Raise the height of the gemstones by sticking them to small pieces of tile with epoxy glue, placing them onto your butterfly design when firmly bonded.

5 Fix the mosaic pieces in place using cement-based adhesive. Make sure you leave gaps of around ⅛in. (3mm) between each tile to allow for the grout. Any awkward pieces can be gently nudged into position with a cocktail stick.

6 When completed, very carefully apply masking tape around the outside of your design to keep the stone clean when you grout the tiles.

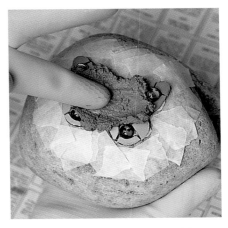

7 Finish by sealing the mosaic with waterproof grout in the usual way (see pages 14–15).

8 If it is difficult to clean out excess grout from any of the nooks and crannies, use a toothbrush to gently ease it away. Remove the tape when the grout has dried.

ladybug stone

you will need:

1 smooth, circular garden stone,
6in. (15 cm) across

32 red glass tiles

6 white glass tiles

22 black glass tiles

3 black ceramic tiles

Pencil and permanent marker

P.V.A.

Tile nippers

Cement-based adhesive

Waterproof grout

Brightly colored ladybugs appeal to all generations and are a welcome visitor to every garden. This project's simple yet effective design is ideal for beginners, and will brighten up any area of your garden. Its base is a garden stone which can be easily bought from any garden center. You may find that the shape of the individual stone dictates the design—some may have a "buglike" look, while others might more closely resemble a caterpillar, or even a flower.

1 First draw your design onto the stone in pencil. When you are completely happy, go over it again with a permanent marker so that it won't run when you later seal the stone.

2 Seal the upper surface of your stone with a solution of 1 part P.V.A. to 3 parts water, and allow to dry.

3 Randomly cut the red and white glass tiles. Nibble circles out of 12 of the black glass tiles and randomly split the rest. Cut the black ceramic tiles, first into quarters, then each quarter into further quarters before dividing them in two to create very small rectangles.

4 Using a cement-based adhesive, carefully lay down your black ceramic pieces in a line over the ladybug's head and down the center of its back. Fill in the eye with your white tiles, making sure that there is a gap between each one, and stick down the ladybug's spots. Use the black glass tiles to mosaic the head, stopping just above where the stone touches the ground, and continue along the ladybug's back in the same manner with the red tiles. When complete, seal the mosaic with a waterproof grout in the usual way (see pages 14–15). Clean and allow to dry.

bird feeder

Birds should always to be encouraged into a garden, and how better than with these decorated feeders? The flat surface of the bird motif is an ideal, if unusual, base for a small mosaic project that can be made in just a few hours. I've loosely based my design on real birds, but feel free to make up your own. Choose your colors according to personal taste, or to complement the natural tones of your garden.

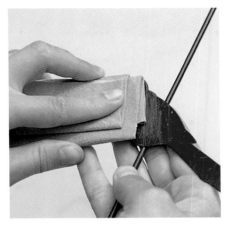

1 Sand down the surface of the bird until it is completely smooth, to help give sufficient grip for the tiles to stick.

2 Draw your design for the mosaic onto the metal bird, indicating the edges of each tile using a marker pen.

you will need:

Hanging bird feeder with metal bird silhouette

8 ceramic tiles of assorted colors

1 imitation gemstone

Sandpaper

Marker pen

Pencil

Tile nippers

Epoxy glue

Cement-based adhesive

Waterproof grout

3 To ensure the mosaic pieces are cut accurately, draw the shapes directly onto the tile using a pencil and nibble away with the tile nippers.

4 To make the eye, use an epoxy glue to stick the imitation gemstone onto a small piece of tile, raising its height . Glue down the tiles with a cement-based adhesive, always remembering to leave a small gap between each tile for the grout. Allow the glue to dry. Finish by sealing the mosaic with waterproof grout (see pages 14–15).

dragonfly

To my mind, dragonflies are some of the most beautiful insects to grace our gardens in the summertime. Their iridescent bodies and lacy wings are so inspiring that I created a larger-than-life version that stays in my garden all summer long. Like the real thing, it shimmers in the sunlight as it floats in the wind beneath my ivy-covered wall, but has the great advantage of never trespassing into my neighbor's garden.

you will need:

Bamboo pole, 24in. (61cm) long

Aluminum mesh, 20 x 6in (51 x 15cm)

10 red iridescent glass tiles

50 green iridescent glass tiles

200 clear iridescent or mirror tiles

3 gold glass tiles

12 black ceramic tiles

Approx. 100 assorted imitation gemstones

Fuse wire

Thick copper wire

Thick garden wire

3 rolls of plaster bandage

Scissors

2 small rubber balls

Metal washer

Cement-based adhesive

Epoxy glue

Tile nippers

Waterproof grout

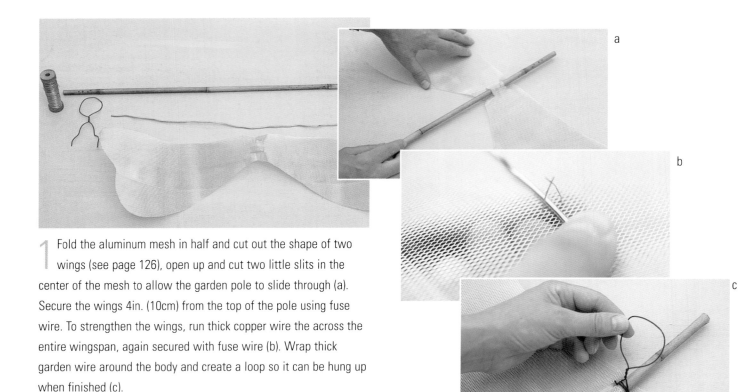

1 Fold the aluminum mesh in half and cut out the shape of two
  wings (see page 126), open up and cut two little slits in the
center of the mesh to allow the garden pole to slide through (a).
Secure the wings 4in. (10cm) from the top of the pole using fuse
wire. To strengthen the wings, run thick copper wire the across the
entire wingspan, again secured with fuse wire (b). Wrap thick
garden wire around the body and create a loop so it can be hung up
when finished (c).

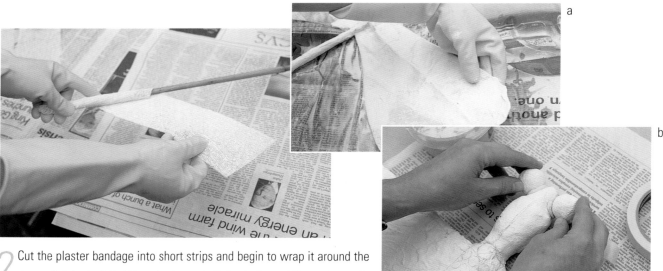

2 Cut the plaster bandage into short strips and begin to wrap it around the
  dragonfly's body. I find it easier to apply it dry, before adding water and
massaging the plaster evenly over the bandage. Put 2 to 3 layers of bandage over
the tail and wings (a), building up the thorax area until it becomes slightly
bulbous. For the eyes, secure 2 small rubber balls wrapped in bandage to eye
sockets with cement-based adhesive (b), place until dry with tape and hold (c).
When the eyes are firmly fixed, reinforce the head area with a strip of plaster
bandage. The plaster will strengthen the structure as well as create a smooth
work surface.

3 Cut 10 red and around 35 of the green tiles into quarters.
Starting at the tail, lay down 4 rows of red tiles among the green
until you reach the body. Work over the front first, allowing the tiles
to dry, before continuing across the back. For the wings, cut the
mirror tiles into small pieces and apply leaving ⅛ in. (3 mm) gaps. To
separate the wings, cut the black ceramic tiles first into 16ths by
quartering quarters and then cut each piece in half, creating small
rectangles which can be laid down in a thin line. Carefully place
imitation gemstones over the eyes. Finally, glue a washer over the
garden wire loop to reinforce the area from which it will be hung.

4 Grout very gently (see pages 14–15)—the unusual
shape requires delicate handling, but with careful
cleaning you'll end up with a stunning result.

TIP

To create the stunning iridescence of the dragonfly,
use colored gemstones, emphasizing their sparkle
by raising their height and combining different-sized
stones. Stick them onto small pieces of tile with
epoxy glue, and, when bonded, attach them to the
body using cement-based adhesive. Make up the
thorax from gold, and red stripes, separated by black
ceramic lines, and the wings from very small
random pieces of iridescent or mirror tiles.
Remember that the tiles on the reverse side can be
larger because they won't be so visible.

MOSAIC LIVING

gingham table top

This brightly colored gingham-effect table top is perfect if you want to revamp an existing piece of garden furniture. With a simple blue-and-white pattern of checkered tiles, this project is ideal for beginners; even the trompe l'oeil details of a summer dragonfly and a lemon slice are simple to create. Although very fresh and contemporary, the inspiration for this piece was a type of Ancient Roman mosaic known as "unswept floor mosaics." The Romans thought food looked so attractive in the aftermath of a great feast that they commissioned mosaics that incorporated scattered food; with trompe l'oeil "fruit" and even the odd "chicken leg" strewn over the tiles.

you will need:

Table for outdoor use

Ceramic and glass tiles:
60 mottled brown ceramic;
240 light blue ceramic;
120 off-white ceramic;
120 dark blue ceramic;
5 yellow ceramic;
2 white ceramic;
1 light yellow glass;
2 green glass;
8 pale gray ceramic;
1 black ceramic;
2 off-white glass; 2 black beads

Permanent marker and pencil

P.V.A. glue

Tile nippers

Exterior wood glue

Waterproof grout

1 Using the templates provided on page 120, draw the lemon and dragonfly motifs onto the table top with a permanent marker.

2 Prepare the wood for the mosaic using a mixture of 1 part P.V.A. to 3 parts water, and allow to dry.

3 Cut the mottled brown tiles in half, and the light blue, dark blue, and off-white tiles into quarters. Place the brown tiles around the outside of the table top, fixed with exterior wood glue. Then lay alternate rows of light blue and white down, and light blue and dark blue tiles to create the gingham tablecloth effect, again using wood glue, leaving gaps for any part tiles around the lemon and insect.

4 To shape the pieces for the lemon slice and dragonfly, draw directly onto the tile with a pencil to help get a precision cut with the tile nippers.

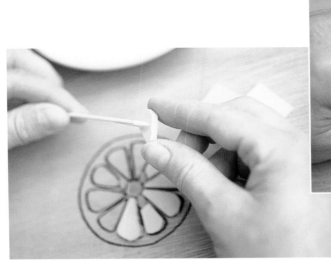

5 Construct the lemon slice from yellow segments surrounded by a circle of white pieces, and centered with a circular glass tile. When finished, insert the part tiles of the surrounding gingham design.

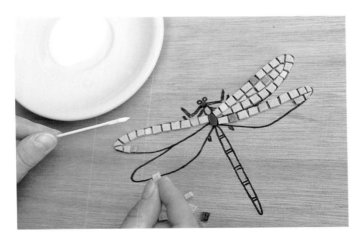

6 The dragonfly's wings are made up of tiles cut into quarters and quartered again, and the eyes are flat-bottomed gemstones. When the table is completely covered with tiles allow to dry before using a waterproof grout in the usual way (see pages 14–15).

honeycomb tray

This project transforms a plain wooden tray into something special. I have a great respect for honeybees, their admirable industry and community, as well as a love of seeing them floating through the garden in summer, and hearing them working tirelessly to collect nectar for the hive. Where better to see them than on the comb as nature intended—working away, producing honey for tea.

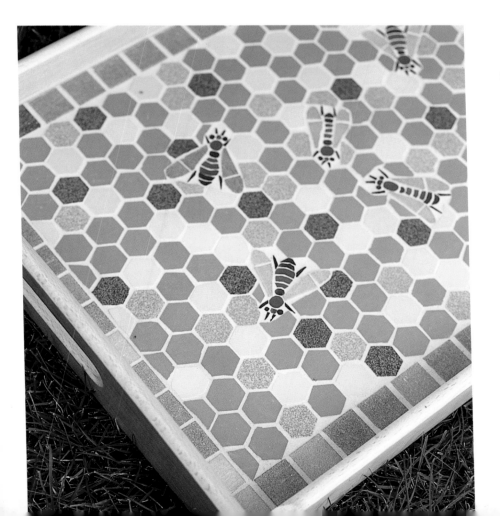

you will need:

Wooden tray

64 assorted honey-colored glass tiles

240 assorted honey-colored ceramic tiles

3 dark brown ceramic tiles

3 light brown ceramic tiles

3 black ceramic tiles

Pen

Pencil

Craft knife

Tile nippers

Wood glue

Waterproof grout

1 Draw the bees onto the tray using the templates provided on page 122.

2 Score the surface of the tray with a craft knife to create more "grip" for the wood glue.

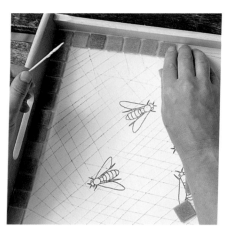

3 Using wood glue, stick down whole glass tiles all around the edge of the tray, ensuring equal gaps are left between each one.

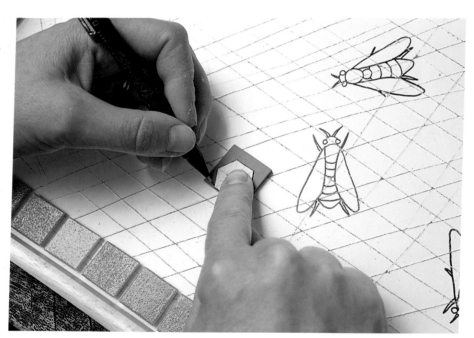

4 Use the template to draw a hexagon onto each honey-colored ceramic tile and cut out using your tile nippers.

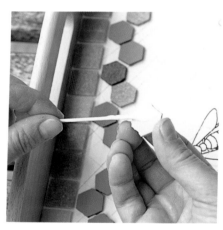

5 To ensure the hexagons are equally spaced, lay down the outside tiles first and then continue into the center of your design, nibbling bits away to allow for the bees.

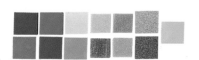

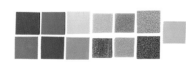

6 Draw the exact shape of each section of the bee onto the remaining ceramic tiles with a pencil before cutting and securing then onto the tray with glue.

7 Finish by filling the gaps between the tiles with grout in the usual way (see pages 14–15).

place mats

The identity of a garden can change quite dramatically with the onset of warmer weather and one of the greatest treats of Spring is "al fresco" eating. From sitting on a blanket to setting the table, the pleasure remains the same. These placemats have been designed specifically for those moments, adding a little extra glamor to the occasion.

you will need:

4 MDF circles, 9in. (23cm) in diameter

Craft knife

P.V.A. glue

60 yellow ceramic tiles

200 assorted white and off-white ceramic tiles

100 glass tiles

Tile nippers

Wood glue

Glue dispenser

Waterproof grout

Acrylic paint

1 Score the wood in a diamond pattern with a craft knife to add some extra "grip" for the tiles when they are stuck down. Without this, the tiles could very easily slip out of place, ruining the overall effect.

2 Prepare the disks by sealing with a mixture of 1 part P.V.A. or wood glue to 3 parts water, and allow to dry. This provides a protective layer between the tiles and base which strengthens the finished piece.

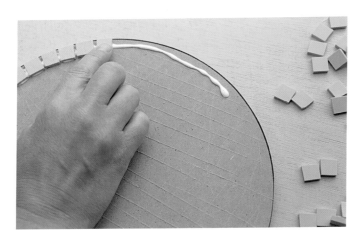

3 Cut the yellow tiles into quarters and stick them with wood glue around the outside of each disk, leaving a gap between each tile.

4 Using a glue dispenser—either freehand or following a pencil line—dispense a swirly line of glue across the center of each placemat. Ensure the line touches the edge twice to create two separate areas.

5 Cut the glass tiles into quarters or 16ths depending on your taste and stick them down along the swirly lines. Cut both the white and off-white tiles into larger, random-shaped pieces and fill each area of the design with a different color.

6 Spread the grout onto the placemats and rub into all the gaps between the tiles. I prefer to do this by hand rather than use a rubber squeegee as it can sometimes dislodge a tile if too little adhesive has been used.

7 When the grout is beginning to dry, start cleaning the excess off with a dry cloth. When the mat is completely clean, paint the edges with acrylic paint in a color of your choice.

coasters

Add to the garden accessories with a set of coasters that can match or contrast with your placemats. They are quick and easy to make—perhaps your children could make their own, or you could have a set that appear on the most special occasions—and will reflect the warmth of a summer evening, and the relaxing atmosphere of a party in the garden.

you will need:

4 plain coasters
28 colored glass tiles
36 off-white ceramic tiles
Tile nippers
Wood glue
Waterproof grout

1 Cut the glass tiles into small squares and rectangles with the tile nippers. The tiles I've cut for the coasters measure around ⅛ in. (3mm) square.

2 Fix them around the outside edge of the coaster using wood glue, alternating the colors.

3 Cut the off-white tiles into small random pieces and position them over the center of the coaster, leaving gaps between each tile.

4 Finish by grouting the mosaic in the usual way (see pages 14–15), taking care to keep the edges clean and smooth. Wipe the underneath of the coaster as well as it may have inadvertently become dirty through handling.

fern plate

The base for this project is a large unglazed terracotta dish, designed to be placed under a plant pot. I've chosen to use it as an interesting alternative to a garden tray, though it would be equally successful as a shallow birdbath, or simply as a decorative plate placed strategically in the garden. My design was influenced by my neighbor's fern and I wanted to demonstrate that even when using just two colors, a mosaic can be eye-catching.

you will need:

Terracotta dish, 16in. (41cm) in diameter

125 green ceramic tiles

140 off-white ceramic tiles

Pencil

Permanent marker

P.V.A.

Tile nippers

Exterior-grade glue

Waterproof grout

1 Draw your design onto the plate with a pencil. When you are completely happy, go over it with a permanent marker.

2 Prepare the plate for mosaic tiling by covering it in a mixture of 1 part P.V.A. to 3 parts water. Allow to dry.

3 Cut the green tiles into quarters and then cut them in half again. Round the edges to create small oblongs that can be glued into place on the bottom leaves and lower stalk. As you work further up the fern, the pattern will get smaller. Cut all of the off-white tiles into quarters and then quarters again. Start by placing them around the fern, cutting any angles that may appear near the tips of each leaf—a method used by the Romans to lift the subject out from the background color. When that is complete, lay the rest of the tiles down in rings, starting from the outer edge, and bring as far into the middle as the design allows, trimming down any tiles that meet the central design.

4 When the base has been completed, glue whole green tiles to the vertical rim of the dish, taking care to space them equally. Allow the glue to dry before grouting in the usual way.

plant shelf

We all have sections of our gardens which need a bit of jazzing up or would benefit from an added splash of color. This project achieves just that in the simplest possible way. This garden shelf is easy to make—no tile cutting is required, and it is easy to install. It rests on four garden bricks, and can easily be put together in an afternoon, to give a perfect base for plant pots and the odd garden sculpture.

you will need:

Plywood plank, 9 x 36in. (23 x 91cm)

256 assorted ceramic tiles

P.V.A.

Exterior wood glue

Waterproof grout

Wood stain

4 bricks

1 Prepare the plywood by sealing with 1 part P.V.A. to 3 parts water and allow to dry.

2 Using wood glue, place your tiles onto the plank, making sure that all the gaps are equal. This is not always as easy as it sounds—it can help to stand back from your work every now and again to check the tiles are running in straight lines. Allow to dry before using a waterproof grout in the usual way (see pages 14–15).

3 Stain the sides and the underneath of the shelf to protect it further against the elements and, when dry, raise it with bricks and place plants on top.

candle holder

During the summer months, the garden assumes many different identities, including that of an extra room for entertaining friends and relations. Good garden lighting helps to set the mood of an occasion, and dotting these candle holders among your plants will look amazing. Their gentle light, glowing in the color of whichever glass tiles you choose to use, will create an atmosphere suffused by calm as the sun sets after a long, hot day.

you will need:

Glass tumbler

4 flat-bottomed glass nuggets

10 blue ceramic tiles

20 pink glass tiles

14 assorted blue glass tiles

Tile nippers

Epoxy resin

Old towel

Waterproof grout

Tea light

1 Cut the blue ceramic tiles into quarters. Cut the pink tiles in half, and then nibble each piece into a point to make a petal shape. Cut the blue glass tiles into random pieces. Working one small area at a time, stick the blue tiles around the top and bottom rims with epoxy resin, making sure they are held in place to dry and don't slip.

2 Dot the glass nuggets around the center of the tumbler, leaving equal gaps between them, and place the pink glass petals around each one. While working, rest the tumbler on an old towel or piece of material, this will hold the piece in place while you work and protect any tiles on the underside.

3 Fill in the surrounding areas with the random fragments of blue glass, and allow the glue to dry.

4 Use a waterproof grout (see pages 14–15) and clean in the usual way. Allow the candle holder to dry fully before placing a tea light inside .

TEMPLATES

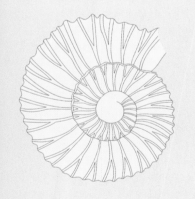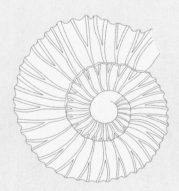

Ammonite Stepping Stone, pages 62–65

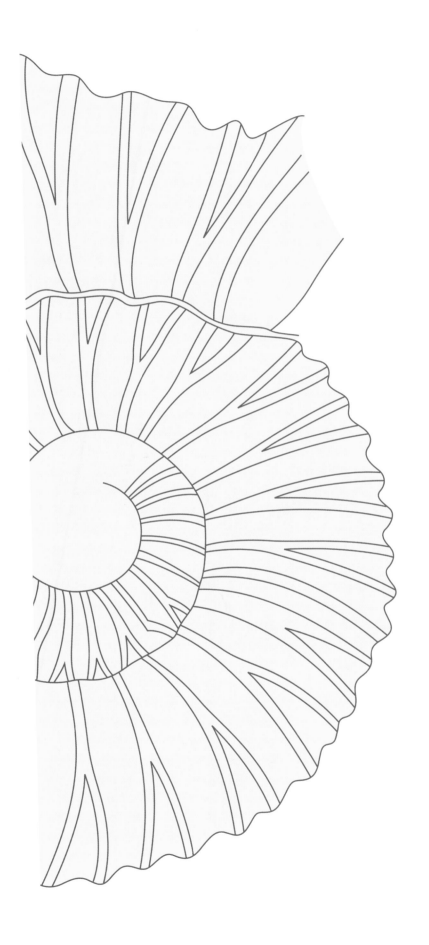

Gingham Table Top, dragonfly, pages 94–97

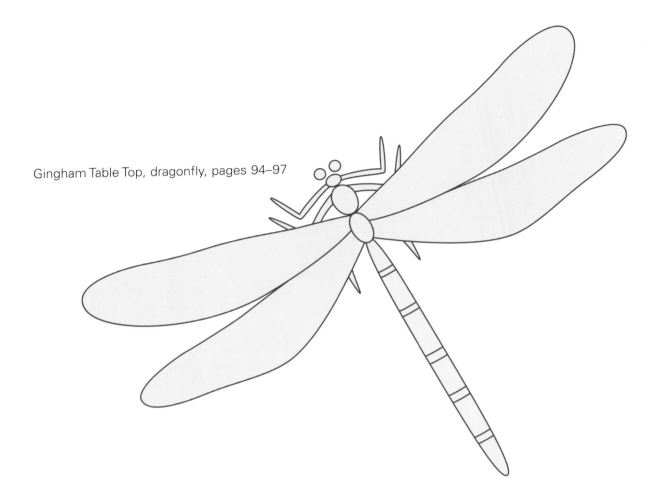

Gingham Table Top, lemon, pages 94–97

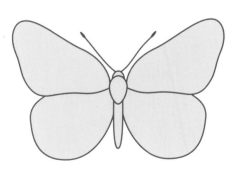

Butterfly on a Stone, pages 80–83

Shoal of Fish, pages 66–71

Children's Footprints, pages 42–47

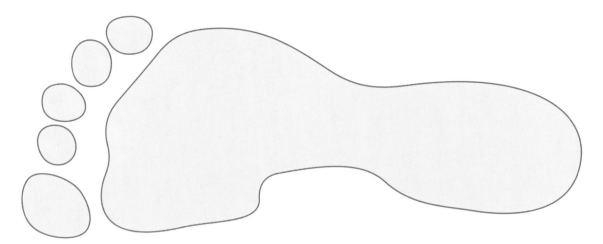

Honeycomb Tray, honeycomb, pages 98–101

Honeycomb Tray, bees, pages 98–101

Ivy-leaf Hanging Pot, pages 22–25
and Ivy Vine, pages 76–79

House Number, numerals, pages 48–51

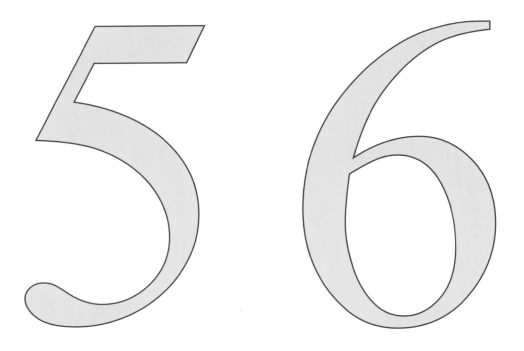

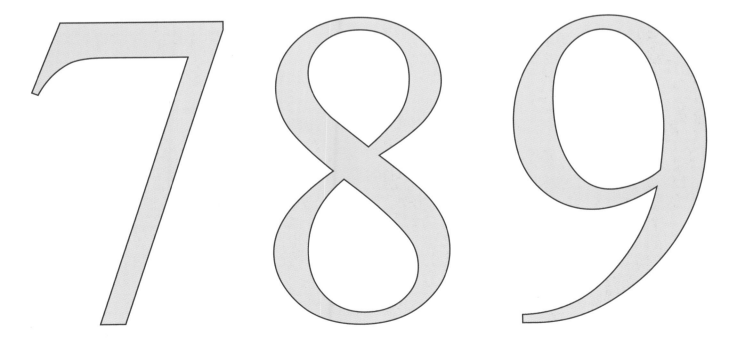

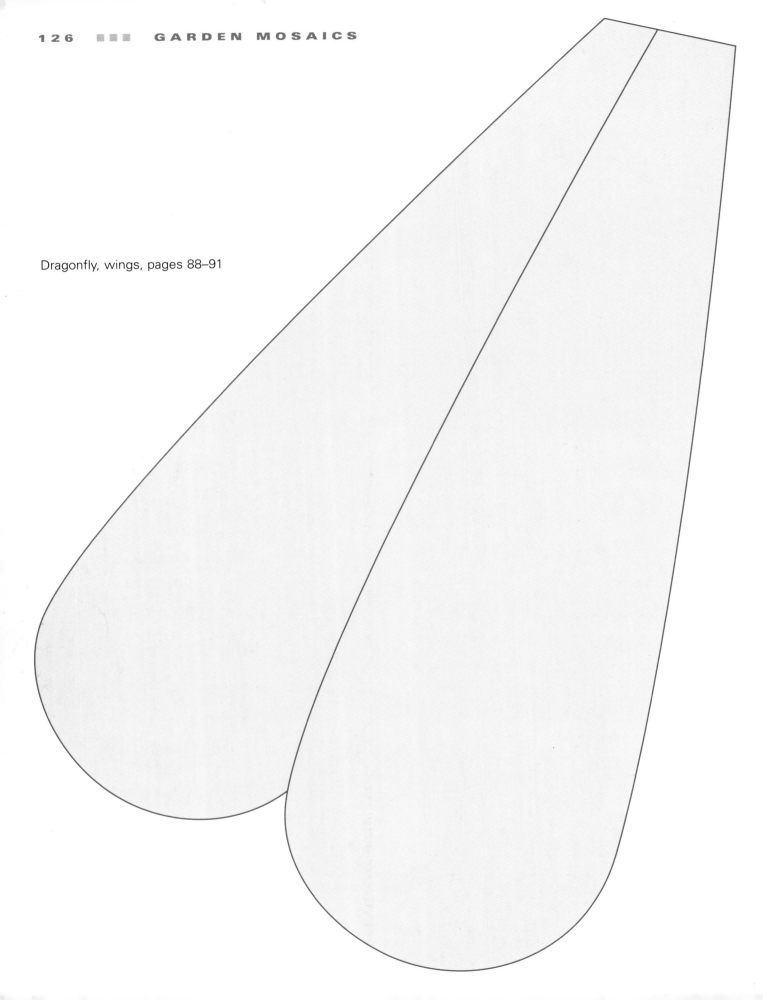

Dragonfly, wings, pages 88–91

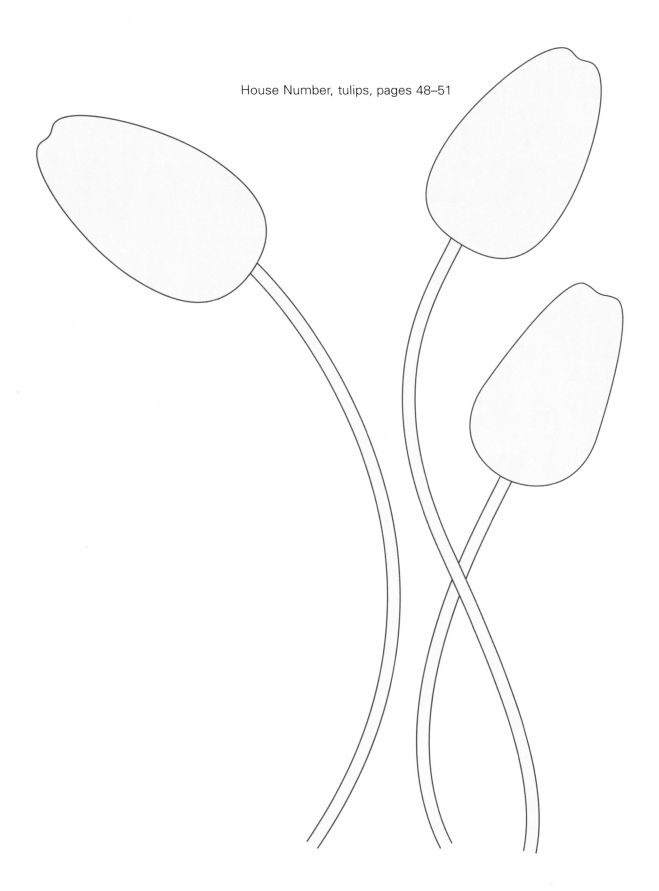

House Number, tulips, pages 48–51

Index

adhesive 13, 19
ammonite stepping stone 62–65
    template 118–119
Art Deco style 51

bee templates 122
birdbath 52–53, 109
bird feeder 86–87
butterfly on a stone 80–83
    template 120

candle holders 33, 112–115
cement, mixing 12
ceramic:
    tiles 8, 11
    two-handled urn 28–31
children's footprints 42–47
    template 122
china tesserae 9
coasters 106–107
concrete recycled planter 26–27
cone planter 32–35
craft knife 19
cutting tiles 10–11

daisy motif 25
dragonfly 88–91, 94–97
    templates 120, 126

fall colors 57
fern plate 108–109
fountain 38–41
fish:
    motif 57
    shoal of 66–71
    sparkling 72–75
footprints, children's 42–47
fossil 9, 62

gemstones 8, 73
gingham table top 94–97
    lemon and dragonfly
        templates 120
glass:
    nuggets 9, 33
    tiles 8, 11
    vitreous 8
glass cutter 16
grout:
    mixing 14
    using 15, 19

hammer and hardy 16
hanging pot, ivy leaf 22–25
honeycomb tray 98–101
    honeybees and honeycomb
        templates 122
house numbers 48–51
    numerals and tulip
        templates 124–125,
        127

ivy-leaf hanging pot 22–25
    templates 123
ivy vine 76–79
    leaf templates 123

ladybug stone 84–85
leaves 23, 123
lemon 94–97
    template 120
light, night 33, 112–115

marble 9
marker pens and pencils 11,
    17
method:
    direct 13
    indirect or reverse 19
millefiori 9
mirror tesserae 9
mixing sand and cement 12

natural materials 9
numerals 48–51
    templates 124–125
nuggets, glass 9, 33

ornamental stone 65

palette knife 13, 16
pathway 42–47
pens and pencils, marker 11,
    17
placemats 102–105
planter:
    concrete, recycled 26–27
    cone 32–35
    fish 67
plant:
    holder 35
    shelf 110–111
plate, fern 108–109
pot
    hanging 22–25
    mosaic 35
    terracotta 15, 109
    tesserae 9
P.V.A. 13, 18, 19

recycled concrete planter
    26–27
rubber gloves 17
rubber squeegee 15, 17

sand 12
sandpaper 17
scoring 18
sealants 18
sealing 18
shelf, plant 110
shells 9
shoal of fish 66–71
    template 121
slurry 12

smalti 9
sparkling fish 72–75
sphere 54–57
spring colors 57
squeegee, rubber 15, 17
staining 18
stepping stone 62–65
stone:
    butterfly on a 80–83
    ladybug 84–85
    ornamental 65
    pierced 39
    stepping 62–65
    tesserae 9
summer 57, 89, 112
summertime sphere 54–57
suncatcher 58–61
syringes 13, 16

table top, gingham 84–97
techniques 10–11, 12, 13, 14,
    15, 18, 19
templates:
    ammonite stepping stone
        118–119
    butterfly on a stone 120
    children's footprint 122
    dragonfly 126
    gingham table top: lemon
        and dragonfly 120
    honeycomb tray:
        honeycomb, bees 122
    house number: numerals
        122–123, tulips 127
    ivy-leaf hanging pot; ivy
        vine: leaves 123
terracotta pot 15, 109
tesserae 8–9
tile nippers 10, 11, 16
tiles:
    ceramic, unglazed 8, 11
    cutting 10–11
    glass 8, 11
tools 16–17
tray, honeycomb 98–101
tulips template 127
two-handled urn 28–31

unglazed ceramic tiles 8
urn, two-handled ceramic
    28–31

varnishing 18
vitreous glass 8

wood glue 13, 18
work space 7
work surface 31

Suppliers

Happycraftn's Mosaic
Supplies
www.happycraftnsmosaicsupp
lies.com
*Multi-colored mirror and
iridescent tiles*

Mosaic Art Supply
www.mosaicartsupply.com
*Large range of mosaics tiles
and tools*

Tessera Glass
www.mosaic-tile.com
Glass and ceramic tiles

Di Mosaico
www.dimosaico.com
Imported Italian tiles

Reed Harris
www.reedharris.co.uk
Ceramic, glass, marble

Mosaic Workshop
www.mymosaicworkshop.co.uk
Glass, ceramic, smalti, marble

Manchester Minerals
www.manchesterminerals.co.uk
Gemstones and imitation gems

The Mosaic Shop
www.themosaicshop.co.uk
*Ceramic, glass, smalti,
pre-cut mirror*

Alec Tiranti
www.tiranti.co.uk
Sculptors' tools and materials

Edgar Udny & Co Ltd
314 Balham High Road
London SW17 7AA
Tel: 020 7767 8181
Glass, smalti, ceramic

Mosaic websites

www.beckymosaics.co.uk
Author's web page

www.americanmosaics.com
American Association
of Mosaics

www.bamm.org.uk
British Association for
Modern Mosaic

www.mosaicmatters.co.uk
Online mosaic magazine